MW00980138

This book is a gift to...

from...

All of the illustrations for this book are original works painted by Veronica Lake in her Portland,
Oregon studio using professional grade watercolor paints on Arches 140 lb paper. Each watercolor
painting is available for purchase as a limited edition Giclee print on watercolor paper, canvas, or
wooden cradle board.

Please visit Veronica's website at: www.impressionsbyveronica.com to purchase art, order additional
copies of the book, or sign up for art classes. You can also contact Veronica via
hushabook@gmail.com or Facebook @Impressionsbyveronica.

Lyrics created by Marilyn Hubler
Arranged by Erik Wright

The New International Version was used as a reference for all scriptures listed.
Copyright © 1986 by Zondervan. All rights reserved. Used by permission.

Designed by Anneli Anderson, designanneli.com

Printed in the United States of America.

ISBN-13: 978-0-692-80171-0

This book is dedicated
to the wonderful parents and children
who helped to make it possible.

Brian and Jolene Bickle
(daughter Katrina)

Scott and Seana Brewer
(son Joseph and daughter Audrey)

Chris and Catie Cambridge
(son Andrew)

Mark and Rachel Heath
(daughter Lydia)

Mitica and Daniela Leontescu
(son Eliav)

John and Bethany Opferman
(daughter Aubrey)

Mark and Christie Sherman
(daughter Penelope)

Joe and Janet Thomas
(daughter Priscilla)

Ben and Katie Walker
(son Timothy and daughter Naomi)

Erik and Amber Wright
(son Chanan)

A special thanks also goes to...

...the countless encouraging people in my life! Their loving reassurance and belief in me, motivated me along. I would like to especially thank Marilyn Hubler for her confidence in me from the beginning. Her vision for this book allowed me to dream big, and she orchestrated a grand selection of children to photograph. Suzanne Frey walked me through each step, and was a great mentor and friend. Crystal Pettit's photographs were particularly appreciated, as I needed just a few more images and she delivered. I also want to thank my dear husband Allen, and Marilyn's husband Craig, who both had the best set of "God looking" hands with which to hold these beautiful children. Most of all, I want to give tribute to my Lord and Savior, Jesus Christ, as I spent countless hours listening as He directed me through each painting, each written word, and every verse. I would never have guessed that I, a simple landscape artist, would ever have the skill to pull this book off – but with God, ALL things are possible ...even this!

Read this beautiful book to your child or
grandchild using the larger, blue lettering.
Download the music for free at:

 https://erik-wright.bandcamp.com/releases

We are all so much like children inside.

Our exterior selves say we are mature adults and able

to handle life. When, however, tragedy strikes, we quickly

realize we are just as vulnerable and saddened as a small

child might be. We all want to find security, love and peace.

Why not find it with the One who knows us best?

Take a seat in your favorite chair and read

the author's words to you.

Take time to find rest for your soul.

*"Be still before the LORD
and wait patiently for Him."*

PSALM 37:7

Hush

A Story for You and Your Child

Written and Illustrated by

Veronica Lake

Hush little baby,
don't you cry.

Have you ever felt like this?

I have. It gives me such comfort knowing God's eyes

are always on me and He is full of compassion.

*"Because of the LORD's great love we are
not consumed, for His compassions never fail.
They are new every morning;
great is Your faithfulness."*

LAMENTATIONS 3:22-23

Your Father in Heaven is by your side.

Resting in the Lord is not a passive activity; only by being intentional will it happen. We have to make a choice. Is God trustworthy enough to go to? Does He really love you? I believe the answer is "yes." If you're not sure, ask Him to reveal Himself. Remind yourself of all the many ways He has taken care of you and blessed you, and then stand firm and BELIEVE. Every request may not result in a "yes," but He promises that He is working all things out for your good. (Romans 8:28) Rest in His promises to you. Here is what God says:

"Do not fear,
for I have redeemed you;
I have summoned you by name;
you are mine!"

ISAIAH 43:1B

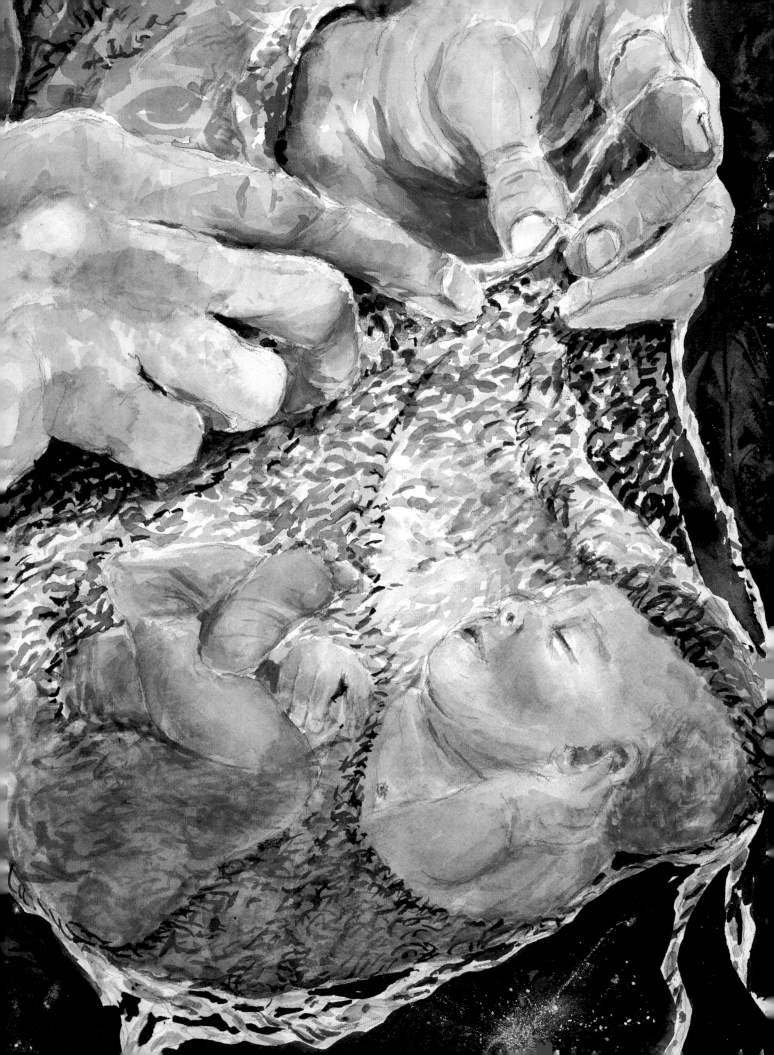

He knew you before your birth;
He made a place for you on earth.

"For you created my inmost being; You knit me together in my mother's womb. I praise you because I am fearfully and wonderfully made."

PSALM 139:13-14

If you and I are knit together by God's loving hands, then there is no mistake about us. Knowing the truth of being carefully thought out and creatively planned brings such wonder to me. Every gift and struggle we face are carefully ordained for a purpose. We can take rest in knowing that God is intimately aware of every aspect of our life. It is even more wonderful to realize that our futures are already written. When we stand before God at the end of the ages, He will have our stories all written there!

"Your eyes saw my unformed body;
and all the days ordained for me
were written in Your book before
one of them came to be."

PSALM 139:16

Hush little baby,
don't you fuss.

We may not see the outcome of our sorrows; but we can choose to rest knowing God loves us, hears us and has good plans for us. Will you choose to trust in God's promise that He loves you and has a hope and future just for you? OR...will you cry and fight like this sweet babe? I know that when I decide to trust, there is such comfort for my soul. Learn to rest....

"For I know the plans I have for you, declares the LORD, plans to prosper you and not to harm you, plans to give you a hope and a future."

JEREMIAH 29:11

You are the gift
He gave to us.

Do you remember looking at your newborn child for the first time? Every toe, finger, and hair so priceless and wonderfully made. In our eyes, our children are the most beautiful beings we have ever seen. Yet, God (the Creator of ALL things) calls us "His children" when we choose to follow Him. We are beautiful in His eyes no matter how sinful, or how unattractive we might think we are. Victorious living is found when we see ourselves the way God does: beautiful, pure and righteous!

We are God's gift.

Simply marvelous to consider!

"For He chose us in Him
before the foundation of the world,
that we would be holy and blameless in His sight.
He predestined us for adoption to sonship
through Jesus Christ, in accordance
with His pleasure and will—"

EPHESIANS 1:4-5

Mommy and Daddy love you so.
We'll protect you as you grow.

It is easy to look into the eyes of our children and want
the very best for them. In our imperfect ways, we nurture
our children; we lead them; and we provide love and safety.
How much more will our Heavenly Father do the same
for us? The questions we must ask are: have we trusted Him?
Have we given up the control of our lives that we seem to
think we have? Can we confidently call upon Him to provide
us with comfort and help even when we don't deserve it?
We can!

"The LORD is near to all
who call on Him, to all who
call on Him in truth."

PSALM 145:18

Hush little baby, no outburst; God is near to heal your hurt.

◦◦◦

When our children cry, we do everything we can to bring them comfort. Wouldn't the God who calls you by name do the same for you? You can rest in the promise that He will hear you and supply your every need. Our God will smile when you simply trust and believe...just quiet your soul...and HUSH.

> *"And my God will meet all your needs according to the riches of His glory in Christ Jesus."*
>
> PHILIPPIANS 4:19

He will keep you in His care; He'll be with you anywhere.

Are you being led by God, or are you still trying to do it on your own? There are no secrets with the One who knows you well. He is trustworthy. We can count on God...even when the answers are sometimes "no," or "wait." Maybe He has something much better than we could imagine!

*"O LORD, you have searched me,
and you know me. You know when I sit and when
I rise; You perceive my thoughts from afar.
You discern my going out and my lying down;
You are familiar with all my ways."*

PSALM 139:1-3

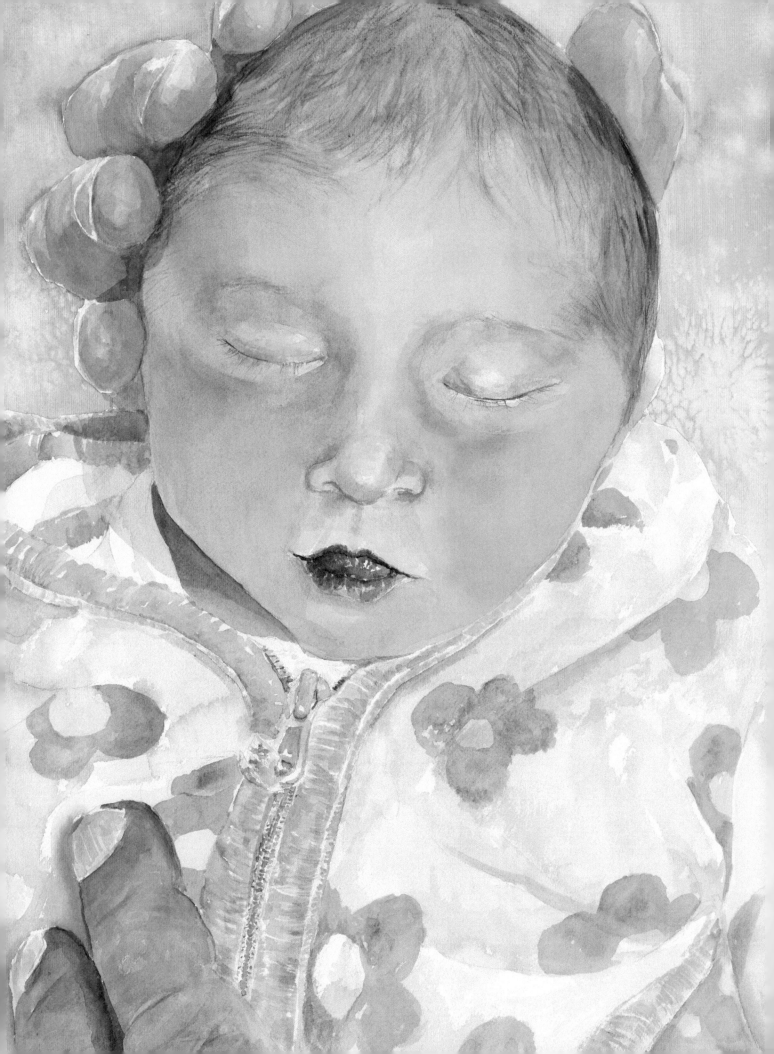

Hush little baby, don't you weep;
God will watch you as you sleep.

I still remember watching the blissful sleep of my infant boys in my arms. I felt overwhelmed with love for them and finally comprehended the great sacrifice God made for me by giving up His ONLY son for me. The reality of that sacrifice became suddenly crystal clear in those quiet moments, in the wee hours of the morning. What a privilege it has been to have children so I could understand this! If we are struggling with life, we can surely find peace when we give our trials over to God.

"I will refresh the weary
and satisfy the faint."

JEREMIAH 31:25

He is strong, yet He is kind.
You are always on His mind.

Can you hear the sound of your laughing child being twirled in your arms? Although my boys are now older, and one is away at college, I remember those times often and cherish each memory. God enjoys us in the same way! His hope is that we will choose to trust Him and find our comfort and hope in a life with Him. Try laughing with your God! After all, He wants us to be joyful!

> *"...may they always say,*
> *'the LORD be exalted, who delights*
> *in the well-being of his servant'."*
>
> PSALM 35:27B

Hush little baby,
don't you shake.

I know there are times that I want to push away from God because things are not going my way. I don't want to give up control. I think I know the answers. Like this young girl, I fight and twist and cry; but God hangs on knowing that He is taking good care of me and looking out for my best interest. God wants me to choose Him and His ways. Do I fight or do I trust?

How about you?

"Trust in the LORD with all your heart
and lean not on your own understanding.
In all your ways submit to Him,
and He will make your paths straight."

PROVERBS 3:5-6

God will guide each step you take.

When I consider that the Lord calls himself a "shepherd"
leading me, I am amazed! Shepherds guide their lambs
to safe pasture and food, they protect them from wild animals,
and will even risk their lives for them. It makes really good
sense to follow, don't you think?

> "The LORD is my shepherd,
> I shall not want. He makes me lie down
> in green pastures; He leads me beside quiet waters.
> He restores my soul; He guides me in paths
> of righteousness for His name's sake. Even though
> I walk through the valley of the shadow of death,
> I fear no evil, for You are with me; Your rod
> and Your staff, they comfort me."
>
> PSALM 23:1-4

He will always be your friend;
He'll be with you to the end.

How comforting it is to know that as a believer,
we are securely in the hands of the great God who made
heaven and earth. Are you searching for hope and answers for
peace? Stop wrestling with God and learn to trust Him also.
If you have never before given your life to God, I can assure
you it is the best decision you will ever make!

The LORD made a promise
to His disciples before He left and went away
into heaven, and it is the same promise He makes
to you and me: "And surely I am with you always,
to the very end of the age."

MATTHEW 28:20B

*For God so loved the world
that He gave His only begotten Son,
that whoever believes in Him shall
not perish, but have eternal life.*

JOHN 3:16

Aren't God's promises and love for us amazing? Now that you have read more about it, why not take the next step? If you are a believer and you are still trying to live life on your own, it might be time for you to renew your commitment to God, and ask Him to take charge? Now is always a good time! Why not talk to God about this right now?

On the other hand, the story of God's love for you might be new. If you don't know God personally, you can chose to walk with Him today! You can say a simple prayer like this:

Lord, I know that I have not been following you. I need your forgiveness. From this day on, I choose to turn from sin and accept Jesus Christ as my personal Savior and Lord. I ask that you would send your Holy Spirit to direct me, fill me, and take control. Thank you that I am your child, and for loving me as my Heavenly Father. Amen.

Be sure to tell someone about your decision to follow Christ Jesus.
I would also love to hear about this! Please email me at hushabook@gmail.com.

27

Being an artist is one of the greatest joys of my life, next to being a mother and wife! Over the last 18 years, I have watched in awe how the Lord has brought work to me and has challenged me to do so many things I believed were not possible. From creating murals high in the air, teaching adults and children of all ages, to illustrating the watercolor paintings for this book, I have learned a great deal with God as my mentor. Through it all, I have had to lean on HIS expertise and wisdom. The Holy Word says we are not permitted to see the face of God and live to tell about it, so I wanted to capture His character by painting loving, powerful and hardworking hands in these watercolors of children. I believe His hands would tell so much about our great God. He is great, powerful, and working for our good!

My greatest aspiration as an artist is to reveal truth to the world in what He has created.

"For since the creation of the world God's invisible qualities—
His eternal power and divine nature—
have been clearly seen, being understood
from what has been made,
so that people are without excuse."

ROMANS 1:20

Endorsements

"I believe the words we speak over our children matter. *Hush* is a captivating book that provides every parent or grandparent the opportunity to speak God's love and hope over their children."

MANDY ARIOTO
President and CEO - MOPS International (Mothers of Preschoolers)

"Weaving poignant scripture verses with magnificent and captivating original paintings, Veronica Lake invites us into a heartfelt conversation while directing our attention to a personal God who has created us in His image and treasures us as His dearly-loved children. *Hush* serves as a beautiful resource to enhance meaningful and truth-filled interactions between parents and children, grandparents and grandchildren."

MICHELLE WATSON, PH.D., L.P.C.,
Author, *"Dad, Here's What I Really Need from You"*

"I love this book! The gentle watercolor washes of babies paired with Veronica Lake's beautiful words make my arms long to hold my own children again. I will purchase this to share with my grandchildren."

JEANNIE ST. JOHN TAYLOR
Best-selling Author / Illustrator of over 25 books for adults and children

"Beautifully painted illustrations with gorgeous words of insight and truth, sure to encourage every heart who reads, and listens to the music. (It comes with a free download of the song.) A "must have" for every parent and grandparent. A perfect gift to give."

SUZANNE FREY
Author, *"Amazing Modern-Day Miracles - 52 True Stories to Strengthen Your Faith"*

"This beautiful and soothing book will capture the hearts of both young and old."

ANN TSEN, MD
Physician Life Development Coach

"As an artist, I'm drawn to the delightful paintings which artist and author Veronica Lake has brought to the pages of this unique and touching book. The paintings of children support inspiring and poetic truths which bring quiet to the child and hushes the heart of the reader. "

JO REIMER
Professional Artist, Teacher, Writer

CPSIA information can be obtained
at www.ICGtesting.com
Printed in the USA
LVXC01n0940151117
556142LV00001BA/1